Facing

Farewell

Face Farewell
with Love,
Knowledge, &
confidence

Dr. Keck

Dr. Julie Reck sitting with Striker, a senior dog given a new home by the Humane Society of Charlotte

Facing Farewell

How and When to Decide Euthanasia for Your Pet

Julie Reck

Doctor of Veterinary Medicine

Cataloging-in-Publication Data is on file with the Library of Congress

ISBN 978-0-557-41627-1

First Edition

This book is dedicated to all the
loving pet owners faced with saying farewell to their
beloved friend

Special thanks to my family for
their lasting support and love
Dr. Julie Reck

"The greatness of a nation and its moral progress can be judged by the way it's animals are treated"

- Ghandi

My Commitment to My Pet and Friend

Your Pet's Name:_____

I love and respect you as a friend and family member. I wish you could be at my side forever, but that it is just not the natural course of the world. I love you enough to let you go when there are no longer means in this world to maintain your comfort and dignity. I will educate myself on all the ways I can help you live comfortably, and when that is no longer an option I will learn how help you gracefully cross to the other side.

With all my love,

_____
Your Name

Table of Contents

"Animals are reliable, many full of love, true in their affections, predictable in their actions, grateful and loyal. Difficult standards for people to live up to."

Alfred A. Montapert quotes

Chapter 1

Introduction

Chapter 1: Introduction

Over the last several decades the role and purpose of the pet in the American household has changed drastically. The pets that were once kept outside for security and rodent control now share our warm beds at night. Our dogs and cats no longer eat solely left over kitchen scraps, rather the family purchases species specific pet food balanced for their nutritional requirements. The American pet has shifted from a servant of the family and now stands as a member of the family.

This shift of purpose and significance has drastically altered medical care and management of our four legged counterparts. New surgeries and treatments enter the veterinary field almost daily. Thanks to pioneers in the profession it is now possible to replace an animal's hip, kidney, and even bone marrow. While my profession has done an excellent job creating ways to "extend" or "improve" the lives of our pets, we are falling short when Americans are faced with saying farewell to their beloved furry family members.

This book is designed to help pet owners gain insight, knowledge, and comfort with the process of pet euthanasia. I recognized fear and misunderstanding of this process when I started "Home Farewell," a mobile veterinary practice that exclusively performs compassionate in-home euthanasia. On a daily basis, I receive a phone call from a pet owner whose soul is genuinely tortured by having to make the difficult choice of euthanasia. When I started Home Farewell I was prepared to help people with the difficult process of home euthanasia, but I was honestly taken aback by the agony and torment my clients experienced over the decision of euthanasia.

To explain my initial surprise I will introduce you to a wonderful dog named Simon. Simon entered my life in the middle of veterinary school. He is a once in lifetime pet and one of my best friends. My relationship with him serves as a daily reminder of why I wanted to be a veterinarian, and he motivates me to be more compassionate and understanding with my patients and clients. We have an exquisite and strong bond that I will never experience with a human. I jokingly tell him that his only job is to live forever, but one day I will likely face the decision of euthanasia for him. I will be grief struck and emotionally devastated for his loss, but I will not experience torture and anguish over my decision to euthanize him. I spent a significant amount of time pondering why a veterinarian can make end of life decisions for her personal pets with less misery and suffering then the average pet owner. This difference resides in knowledge and familiarity. I have been trained to recognize animal pain, I understand when no further medical options exist for a disease, and I know the procedure and drugs of euthanasia. I cannot provide you a veterinary degree in this book, but I can provide you the comprehensive information on the process of euthanasia that you deserve as a pet owner.

I run Home Farewell on the basis that, "*saying farewell should be the hardest part.*" It is my hope that after reading this book you will be empowered with knowledge and perspective, so when you are *facing farewell* with your pet "saying farewell" will be harder for you then "deciding farewell."

"If having a soul means being able to feel love and loyalty and gratitude, then animals are better off than a lot of humans."
- James Herriot

Chapter 2

Human and Animal Perspectives on Life and Death

Chapter 2: Human and Animal Perspective

on Life and Death

As a culture we are guilty of interacting and caring for our animals in an anthropomorphic manner. We (including myself at times), often view our pets as our children providing them with toys, play dates, and even clothes. In my experience as a veterinarian, a reasonable attachment and association of human-like qualities on our animals is generally harmless and can encourage compassion toward the animal kingdom. While attaching human characteristics to our pets can strengthen our human-animal bond, it is critically important to not impose our human perspective and fears associated with death on our beloved animals.

I chose to begin this book with a discussion of the difference between the human and animal perspectives on life and death to help the pet owner make rationale, compassionate end of life decisions for their pets without the insertion of human contrived fear and angst toward death. All creatures have a day of birth and a day of death. Humans uniquely perceive a straight timeline between birth and death and strive for the timeline to be as long as possible. From early childhood we are instilled with the need to achieve goals and life accomplishments. We seek education, career, adventure, and the formation of our own family. Our species has had a long fascination with retaining youth and seeking immortality. Throughout our lives we can always find something to live for: weddings, births, or unachieved ambitions. We fear the concept that the world will continue to function without us. These perceptions and apprehensions are uniquely human and are not shared by our animal companions.

Like us animals are given a day of birth and a day of death, but unlike us their lifespan is not linear but circular. Initially they are young, then they mature, and with time they age. Pets do not fear any stages of life and receive the onset of a grey muzzle and stiff joints with grace. My experience as a veterinarian has provided me with the wisdom that *animals do not fear death, but they do fear pain.* I really absorbed this concept a few months after beginning Home Farewell, my mobile home euthanasia veterinary practice. During the process of scheduling a home euthanasia pet owners frequently ask if they should restrict the other household animals from the euthanasia area. In the beginning, I did not have solid advice but often encouraged owners to allow the other pets to have access to the euthanasia area so long as they did not upset the patient or disturb the process. The other pets rarely were disruptive and their response to the situation and the loss of their housemate was often astounding. In almost all instances the other household animals acknowledge the deceased. They do not seem to be fearful of the situation and express an understanding of the housemate's passing. Two memories from home euthanasia appointments deserve sharing and reveal our animal's sentiment toward passing away.

The first memory involves a family with two cats, one male cat and one female cat. The female cat was diagnosed with liver and kidney failure over a weekend at an emergency clinic. She was stabilized at the hospital but the emergency vet informed the owners that she would only remain stable and comfortable for 48 hours outside the hospital. The family elected to allow their cat to enjoy the comforts of her home for one more day and decided to have her euthanized at home. When I arrived at the family's house, I found them on the back porch holding and petting their very ill female cat. As soon as I set my bag down by the family, a robust male cat walked toward me. He demanded my attention, and once I diverted my focus to another person or task he loudly meowed. He seemed insensitive and unaware that his housemate was ill, and he grew bored with the steps of the euthanasia procedure. He was not restricted from the porch, but he elected to play with his cat toys in the living room while his owners said goodbye to his housemate. After she passed away and the goodbyes were finished, I wrapped her in a towel and my husband, who often assists me on my home euthanasia procedures, gathered all our medical equipment. As I was carrying her through the house, I stopped to ask the family if they wanted their male cat to have an opportunity to see her and say goodbye. They paused for a moment in thought, and he suddenly appeared at my feet. I took it upon myself to kneel down while holding the female cat. The male placed his front paws on my lap to look at what I was holding. After a quick glance, he began to turn away only to change his mind and take a second look. He stood higher on my lap and placed his face right up to his housemate's. Their noses touched for about 3 seconds and he pressed his head against hers. He stepped off my lap then definitively walked away and sought his toys again. He played with his toy mouse as if nothing had happened. I was completely astounded for a moment, then rose and continued to head toward the car. I said goodbye to the family and entered the passenger side. We began to drive away and I looked over at Matt. He was very silent and his eyes tearful. In the house, he was standing next to me and fully witnessed the feline goodbye. I was searching for something to say to him. "I told you they know," I stated. After a moment he said, "I got that now."

The second memory surrounds a family with a Golden Retriever and a cat. The cat suffered from liver disease that caused fluid to build up in his abdomen. The Golden Retriever was used as a therapy dog visiting senior citizens in the hospital. Eight family members surrounded the cat during his euthanasia procedure. Each person said their individual goodbyes and shared their favorite memory with their feline friend. As he passed away the family members became very emotional. The Retriever was lying on the floor across the room. The tears and sobbing of the family prompted him to stand up and walk to the deceased feline. He laid down next to the cat and placed his head over the body. The family was overwhelmed by the dog's actions. After a few minutes, he stood up and approached each family member individually. He placed his head on their lap and stayed until they seemed comforted by his presence. The Retriever recognized the passing of his feline housemate and was content that he was no longer in pain. He was not afraid of the feline's death, and he clearly wanted to support his family so they would be more comfortable with the passing of their beloved cat.

These memories highlight that the animals that are present at the death of their housemate do not exhibit fear or anxiety toward the situation. They are capable of understanding that their counterpart is no longer uncomfortable or suffering. As we are faced with end of life choices for our pets it is very important that we discard the human perception of life and death, and base our decision on the animal's perspective on life and death. Keeping this mindset will provide comfort and confidence when you are faced with saying farewell to your pet.

"Dogs are not our whole life, but they make our lives whole."
Roger Caras quotes

The following worksheet will help you recognize your
own perspective on living and dying. It will also allow
you reflect on your pet's current stage of life

Human and Animal Perspective on Life and Death
Worksheet

A. Do you fear pain for yourself? _____yes _____No

B. Do you fear dying? _____Yes _____No

C. Given the choice how long would you want to live in years?

_____yrs

D. Please write the age of your pet in years and their species:

Age_____ yrs Species_____

E. By either consulting with your regular veterinarian, internet research, or reading breed specific books please write the average lifespan of your pet based on species and breed:

_____ average lifespan in yrs

F. Please use the charts located on page 22 and 23 to find your
pets actual age into human years:

        human age of your pet   _____yrs

G. Compare the results from option "C" with option "F." In some
cases the numbers will be very similar. Take a moment to reflect on the
comparison of human and animal ages.

Notes/Feelings:_____

_____

_____

_____

_____

_____

_____

_____

_____

_____

_____

_____

Human Age of Dogs

Giant Breeds of dogs have a different lifespan than toy breeds. Find your dog's human age by his or her weight

Actual Age	0-15 pounds	16-50 pounds	51-80 pounds	> 80 pounds
1-11 mo	Pediatric	Pediatric	Pediatric	Pediatric
1 year	6 year old	7 year old	8 year old	10 year old
2 year	12 year old	13 year old	15 year old	20 year old
3 year	19 year old	22 year old	28 year old	35 year old
4 year	25 year old	28 year old	34 year old	45 year old
5 year	32 year old	37 year old	45 year old	55 year old
6 year	38 year old	44 year old	55 yea old	65 year old
7 year	45 year old	50 year old	63 year old	75 year old
8 year	51 year old	58 year old	70 year old	85 year old
9 year	58 year old	63 year old	77 year old	95 year old
10 year	65 year old	70 year old	82 year old	105 year old
11 year	68 year old	75 year old	86 year old	
12 year	71 year old	78 year old	90 year old	
13 year	75 year old	82 year old	95 year old	
14 year	78 year old	86 year old	100 year old	
15 year	80 year old	90 year old	105 year old	
16 year	83 year old	95 year old		
17 year	85 year old	100 year old		
18 year	88 year old	105 year old		
19 year	91 year old			
> 20 year	95 year old			

Human Age of Cats

Stage of Life	Actual Age in Years	Human Age
PEDIATRIC	0-11 months	5 year old
	1 year	10 year old
ADULT	2 year	14 year old
	3 year	22 year old
	4 year	27 year old
	5 year	32 year old
	6 year	37 year old
MIDDLE AGE	7 year	44 year old
	8 year	50 year old
	9 year	55 year old
	10 year	58 year old
	11 year	62 year old
SENIOR	12 year	66 year old
	13 year	70 year old
	14 year	74 year old
	15 year	78 year old
	16 year	82 year old
GERIATRIC	17 year	86 year old
	18 year	90 year old
	19 year	95 year old
	20 year	100 year old
	21 year	103 year old
	22 year	105 year old

"Animals have these advantages over man: they never hear the clock strike, they die without any idea of death, they have no theologians to instruct them, their last moments are not disturbed by unwelcome and unpleasant ceremonies, their funerals cost them nothing, and no one starts lawsuits over their wills."

Voltaire

Chapter 3

The Euthanasia Procedure

Making sure it's done right

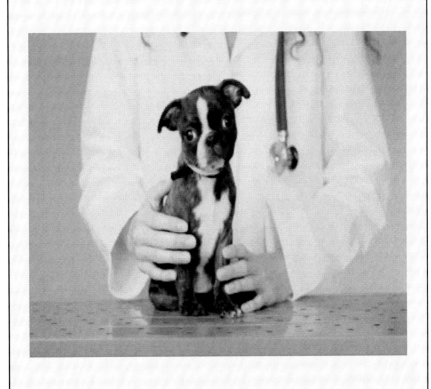

Chapter 3: The Euthanasia Procedure:

Making sure it is done right

With an understanding of the difference between human and animal perceptions of life and death, an in depth discussion of the techniques of humane euthanasia is warranted. This will likely be the most challenging chapter for the pet owner to complete, but it is certainly the most important. Anyone faced with the decision of euthanasia will benefit from a complete understanding of euthanasia as a medical procedure. People fear what they do not know or understand; therefore, discussing the procedure of euthanasia early in this book can reduce apprehension over the actual euthanasia procedure assisting pet owners in their decision making.

When talking to others who have faced this situation in the past, you will hear stories that it was a peaceful experience for the animal and everyone who witnessed. You will also encounter stories in which owners felt the euthanasia did not go peacefully and they suspected the animal felt pain or discomfort during the procedure. This will be a truthful discussion of the techniques and protocols of humane euthanasia, and it will dispel common myths of the procedure. At the conclusion of this chapter you will find yourself fully educated on the process of euthanasia, which will allow you to be an informed medical advocate for your pet. As a veterinarian, I have found comfort in understanding the mechanics and medications of euthanasia. It is my hope that providing pet owners with the same understanding and education will also provide them the same comfort.

The stages of euthanasia and common questions regarding the process will be discussed in a step by step manner.

I'm Scared!

I want to be there for my pet, but I don't know if I can handle watching the procedure

---

It is normal to be fearful or anxious of the euthanasia procedure. In our day to day lives, we normally do not encounter death or the dying process. Most of us have never seen another animal or human pass away. I too was initially very frightened by this process. In veterinary school, your education is focused on recognizing the symptoms of diseases and applying treatments to animals to save their life. Depending on the cases and patients a student works with in their clinical rotations, it is possible to only witness a handful of euthanasias before becoming a doctor. In fact, I will share the story of the first euthanasia I performed as a doctor just out of vet school.

On my third day as a practicing veterinarian, the receptionist scheduled my first euthanasia appointment. An hour before the appointment, I began feeling a bit nervous and arranged all the supplies I would need for the procedure. The pet was a 17 year old dog that was suffering from several medical issues, the most severe being a "Parkinson-like" syndrome that was affecting her nervous system. She had a very difficult time standing and had lost the ability to walk. She had a persistent body wide twitch due to the neurologic condition. Her owner was a nurse and had experienced several euthanasia appointments with her pets in the past. I gathered the supplies into the exam room and we began the steps of the euthanasia procedure. I placed an IV (in the vein) catheter into the pet's front arm to ensure that when the euthanasia solution was administered, all the medication would enter the bloodstream. It was difficult to place the catheter because the pet was having the involuntary muscle twitches, but because of the owner's medical background she was very helpful and understanding of the difficulties I was experiencing. Once the catheter was in place and all the goodbyes were said, I began to administer the euthanasia solution into the IV catheter. It is important that all the medication be delivered to the bloodstream quickly, because the medication only takes a few seconds to be effective. When I was at the half way point, her muscle twitching became suddenly worse and her arm with the IV catheter jerked away from me. I remained focused and knew I had to act quickly to ensure that this wonderful and loved pet would have a peaceful passing. Within a split second, I had the needle and syringe back into the IV catheter and began to administer the remainder of the euthanasia solution. A few moments later, I realized that instead of placing the needle into the catheter I had accidentally placed in my left thumb and had injected some of the medication into myself! Once again, I maintained my focus and replaced the needle into the IV catheter. This time it was definitely in the correct place and in the next second the pet peacefully passed away. Being a nurse, the owner did not miss that I injected myself with a small amount of the solution. "Thank you so much for your composure and helping her go peacefully, but I am really concerned…Are you going to be ok?" I stared at my thumb with a wide eyed gaze and said, "I am not sure." I stepped out of the room and asked the other vets in the hospital if this had ever happened to them and if they thought I needed to seek medical attention. After a few minutes, I became dizzy and threw up (which was likely from anxiety I was having over the situation), but obviously I am fine. I am telling you this story not to frighten you or increase your worries that something may not go well during the procedure. The events that happened during that procedure were a fluke, once in a lifetime occurrence. Such unpredictable events like that have never happened to me since, nor to any other vet that I know. The moral of my story is that my fears and anxieties with euthanasia and death have dissipated thanks to the experience and knowledge I have gained with the procedure. Who would have thought that the young doctor that gave herself part of the medication during her first euthanasia appointment would go on to dedicate her career to that aspect of veterinary medicine? I encourage you to go through the following information on the euthanasia procedure as many times as you need to gain comfort with this process. Gaining this knowledge will give you the confidence you need to be by your pet's side. Trust me, I'm <u>Living Proof</u> of it!!

What is the euthanasia medication?
&
How does it work?

The term "euthanasia" stems from the Greek language and is translated to "good death." It is defined by experts of medical ethics as "a deliberate intervention undertaken with the express intention of ending a life, to relieve intractable suffering." The most humane way to perform animal euthanasia is by injecting the proper medication intravenously (or into the vein, IV). Other methods of euthanasia (such as oral medications, inhaling gases, or injections into the skin/muscle) will not be included in the discussion and are generally not administered to companion animals with owners. The procedure is best performed by a licensed veterinarian and sodium pentobarbital is the most common medication. Sodium pentobarbital was created in 1928 as an agent for anesthesia. Scientists quickly discovered that a small overdose of sodium pentobarbital did not increase the length of time a patient would stay under anesthesia but caused rapid unconsciousness followed by respiratory arrest. Within seconds of respiratory arrest, cardiac function stops and death occurs.

Is animal euthanasia the same lethal injection given to prisoners?

Many pet owners are curious if the same medications and protocols that are used for human lethal injections are used for animal euthanasia. As of 2010, this is a highly controversial topic and most states have made it illegal for veterinarians to use the same medications used in human executions. Most human executions are performed by a series of 3 medications. Thiopental is the initial medication and causes the inmate to be placed under general anesthesia. The second medication causes paralysis but does not cause loss of consciousness. The final medication is potassium chloride which interrupts the heart's electrical function and causes the organ to seize up. Potassium chloride is reported to be extremely painful when given to patients that are not in a deep plane of anesthesia. It is argued that the administration of the paralyzing agent may prevent a prisoner from communicating that the dosage of the initial medication was not sufficient to produce deep anesthesia. If this were to occur, then the prisoner would feel severe pain during the final injection but would be unable to move or communicate due to the second injection. Some judicial officials argue that there is the potential for a death row prisoner to suffer cruel and unusual punishment with this combination of medications. Veterinarians rarely administer a paralyzing agent because the most common animal euthanasia agent is an extremely large overdose of anesthesia that is painless when given intravenously, rather than potassium chloride.

The Steps of the Euthanasia Procedure

With an understanding of the difference between lethal injection and animal euthanasia, it is time to discuss optimal protocols to conduct a humane and peaceful animal euthanasia. As mentioned in the previous paragraph, it is essential that the entire dose of sodium pentobarbital for the animal's weight be administered intravenously to produce a rapid, painless euthanasia. Failure of part of the medication to entire the bloodstream could produce a catastrophic and inhumane outcome. How can an owner guarantee that their pet will receive all the euthanasia medication into the bloodstream? The safest solution is to request that the veterinarian place an IV catheter a few minutes before the procedure. The owner should expect a small increase in the euthanasia fee when an IV catheter is placed to cover the expense of the veterinarian's equipment and supplies (in 2010, average IV catheter cost for a pet owner is $30-$40). This expense is advantageous to ensure that your pet's procedure in performed safely and humanely.

      As a you read and understand the importance of placing an IV catheter prior to administering the euthanasia solution, you may be concerned that your pet will find the IV catheter placement painful or frightening. As a veterinarian, I share this concern and feel reducing a pet's fear and anxiety is part of conducting a humane euthanasia. In gaining clinical experience with the euthanasia procedure, I also grew uncomfortable administering the sodium pentobarbital to fully awake, unsedated patients. While the euthanasia solution works very rapidly, there is a split second that the animal realizes it is losing control of its consciousness. I know the patient is not experiencing pain during that split second, but I do predict that the pet experiences a moment of anxiety. It is for these reasons that I provide my patients with sedation/pain medication prior to placing the IV catheter or administering the euthanasia solution. At my home euthanasia appointments, administering the sedation is the first course of action I take once the family and pet have become comfortable with my arrival. The sedation is given as an injection under the skin and is the same volume and needle size as the pet's yearly vaccinations. I give the injection in the shoulder area because the pet loses its peripheral line of sight in this area and does not visualize the needle. The owner is aware of the injection and tasty treats are dropped in front of the animal to distract them from the brief and mild discomfort of the injection. (Please note that animals can react unpredictably during an injection, owners should follow their veterinarian's suggestions to avoid personal injury). Most pets will have a slight flinch as the injection is given, just as they would for a vaccine. In my experience, by the time the pet realized they received a shot it is all over and the sedation is able to take effect. If you would prefer that your animal receive sedation as a first step in the euthanasia procedure, then arrange a discussion with your veterinarian prior to your euthanasia appointment. Your veterinarian likely has a tremendous amount of experience with a variety of sedation options, he or she will be well suited to select a sedation agent based on your pets species, age, and medical condition. Sedation medications are generally very expensive for the veterinarian to purchase, and it would be normal for the veterinarian to charge 15-25% more for the euthanasia fee when sedation is given as the initial step.

If you have selected sedation and an IV catheter, then your pet will be sleeping soundly and will be prepared to receive the euthanasia solution in a safe, humane manner. The veterinarian will likely ensure that the catheter is functioning properly with sterile water or saline, and then they will inject the final euthanasia solution directly into the IV catheter. It is important the pet owner anticipate that the pet will pass away as the medication is administered or a few seconds after the injection is completed. The actual euthanasia is very rapid and pet owners can become upset if they are not prepared for the prompt nature of the medication.

What happens after the procedure?

The veterinarian will use a stethoscope to ensure that the heart has stopped beating, after which he or she will pronounce the pet as deceased. Pet owners will benefit from remembering sodium pentobarbital's mode of action. It first causes loss of consciousness, then stops respiration, and finally stops the heart. It will take the muscles and nervous system a few minutes to completely use the remaining energy left in the cells, despite the fact that the heart is no longer beating. This is why it is normal to witness a twitch of the leg or lip a few minutes after the vet confirmed that the pet no longer has a heartbeat. The chest may rise and fall several times and it may appear that the pet is breathing. The pet is not breathing to intake air, it is just the energy escaping from the muscles that are used to take a breath.

Animals have different conformation of their eyelids when compared to humans. Humans have soft, flaccid upper eyelids that require energy from muscles in the upper lid to remain open. Animals have more taunt upper lids that require muscle energy when fully open and closed. Because of the anatomy of their eyelids, most animals pass away with their eyes half open.

Most owners spend a few minutes with the pet after it passes away. These moments provide owners with closure and peace of mind that the animal is relieved of its suffering. As the minutes progress, and the energy dissipates from the muscles defecation and urination may occur. If excretion does occur it usually happens 5-10 minutes after the pet passes away. If the animal was suffering a medical disease specifically related to the urinary or intestinal systems, then urination or defecation can occur immediately after the pet passes away.

It is advised to decide on an option for your pet's remains before the euthanasia appointment. You will be overwhelmed with emotions after you lose your pet and it will be comforting to have the arrangements completed. Some owners will elect a burial option either on their property or in a pet cemetery. If you elect this option remember to prepare your vehicle ahead of time. Place heavy duty plastic under the animal and bring a large blanket to cover your pet. This will reduce odor and damage to your vehicle during transport. If burial is not an option, then most pet owners select cremation. Pet cremation services usually offer two options: individual or communal cremation. During an individual cremation the animal is placed into the incinerator alone, and the process allows the pet owner to receive their pet's specific ashes. If a pet owner does not wish to receive their pet's ashes, then communal cremation with other pets is a more economical option. Your veterinarian will likely have an existing relationship with a pet cremation service in your community. The cremation service generally will pick up your pet directly from your vet's office or your home.

Acquiring an understanding of the process of euthanasia as a medical procedure can be a difficult and emotional course. When a pet owner is informed and prepared there is a greater likelihood that they will be satisfied that their pet peacefully passed away and will have confidence in their decisions. It is important that owners select the veterinarian and the procedure options for their pet's euthanasia based on their emotional connection with the person and the process rather than the cost. Americans are driven to seek deals and save money, but they should avoid this mindset when making end of life decisions for their pet. Saving fifty dollars will not seem important, if the euthanasia protocol does not eliminate the pet's anxiety and discomfort during the process.

Checklist for the Steps of Compassionate Euthanasia

✓ SEDATION

An injection is given under the skin that will progressively cause the pet to fall into a deep sleep

✓ IV CATHETER

A small plastic tube is placed by the vet or staff into the blood vessel. It is secured in place with tape and saline is injected into the catheter to make sure it functions properly

✓ EUTHANASIA SOLUTION GIVEN INTO CATHETER

The euthanasia solution is administered into the bloodstream via the IV catheter. The pet passes away within a few seconds after the injection is complete.

Take a moment to fill out the following worksheet and consider options you would like you pet to receive during the euthanasia procedure. This can be an excellent outline for a discussion between you and your veterinarian before the euthanasia procedure.

The Euthanasia Procedure Worksheet

A. Do you want your pet to have the euthanasia medication administered into an IV catheter to ensure all the medication enters the bloodstream?

Yes_____   No_____

B. Do you want your pet to receive sedation as the first step in the euthanasia procedure?

Yes_____   No_____

If Yes, then discuss the best sedation option for your pet with your veterinarian

Name of Sedation:_____

Notes about the sedation:_____

_____

_____

Be sure to ask how **long** it takes for the sedation to work, **how sedate** will the animal become, will they feel any **pain**, what is the **cost**....Remember the more informed you are about the process, then the more confident you will be that you have made the best decisions for your pet

C. Will your pet be receiving sodium pentobarbital as the euthanasia agent?

Yes_____   No_____

If your vet has not selected this medication have a discussion before the euthanasia appointment about the euthanasia medication. He or she may have specific reasons for selecting an alternative euthanasia agent

D. How do you want to handle your pet's remains:

    a. Burial_____

           i. If you need assistance with preparing the burial site be sure to arrange this ahead of time. Pet cremation services will often prepare the burial site for a fee. Research HOA and government restrictions and be sure that at least 18 inches of soil covers the animal

    b. Cremation

           i. Communal_____

               Cost_____

          ii. Individual _____

               Cost_____

               1. most cremation services offer a selection of urns, they can be selected be or after the pet has been euthanized.

Notes from your discussion with your veterinarian about the steps that will be taken during your pet's euthanasia procedure:

_____

_____

_____

_____

_____

_____

_____

_____

Lots of people talk to animals.... Not very many listen, though.... That's the problem.

~Benjamin Hoff, *The Tao of Pooh*

Chapter 4

Animal Pain

How can you tell?

Chapter 4: Animal Pain....How can you tell?

Armed with the animal perspectives of life and death and familiarity with euthanasia as a medical procedure, pet owners can focus on how to recognize the symptoms of pain in their pet. For most pet owners it is heartbreaking and unacceptable to witness a beloved friend in pain. Animals lack the ability to speak our oral language; therefore, we feel compelled to serve as their advocate for preventing, controlling, and ending their pain. The veterinary profession and animal divisions of pharmaceutical companies have greatly increased the options available for pain management in pets. Once pain is identified, your veterinarian will be a valuable expert on medications to manage your pet's pain and will help you define the circumstances in which medications or procedures no longer exist to alleviate your friend's pain. However, the most difficult part of this process is often recognizing that your animal is in pain and the level of discomfort they are experiencing. Despite being domesticated species that share our homes, our pets still rely heavily on their instincts, and it is often their instinct to hide pain and illness as long as possible. This chapter is designed to help your recognize body changes and symptoms of pain that animals will display when they are in their home. Your veterinarian is proficient in diagnosing pain in animals, but he or she is at a disadvantage. The fear and anxiety that most pets experience at the veterinary clinic can disguise symptoms of pain. Being educated on the symptoms of animal pain will allow you and your veterinarian to work as a team to keep your pet as comfortable and as pain free as possible.

Because of inherent behavioral and physical differences between the canine and feline species their symptoms of pain will be discussed in separate sections

Recognizing pain in dogs

Throughout the process of observing your pet for symptoms of pain a reoccurring theme will appear. With each symptom under consideration it will be important to compare it to how the dog behaved or appeared throughout its life before he or she became sick or old. Consider the example of a dog's appetite. Labrador Retrievers are infamous for having a voracious appetite, and a food loving lab that refuses a meal for the first time may be experiencing pain from an underlying serious illness. On the other hand, toy poodles are often finicky eaters and missing a meal may not be a major clinical symptom of pain for that pet. It is important to consider your pet's normal attitude, behavior, and expressions when deciding if they are displaying symptoms of pain.

Pain symptoms displayed in dogs will be systematically discussed beginning at the head of the dog and continuing toward the tail. Starting at the dog's muzzle, a change in vocalization or barking may indicate pain. A painful dog may show an increase in whining, groaning, or whimpering. The pet may begin barking at people that attempt to come near it. A pet that is usually friendly and vocal when greeted by people, may become shy and quiet when in pain. An abrupt increase in drooling can be a symptom of nausea or visceral (intestinal) pain. A reduction of appetite can be a symptom of pain not only in the GI tract but anywhere in the dog's body. Painful dogs may develop changes in their eyes or facial expression. Severe pain can sometimes cause dilation or widening of the pupil (center black circle of the dog's eye). The pupil is intended to control the amount of light that enters the eye. In sunlight or bright indoor light, the pupil will be small because there is a surplus of light. In a dimly lit space the pupil will be larger to allow more light to the back of the eye. Pet owners need to observe how their pet's eye changes in multiple light settings. If the pet's pupil is very large in a well lit space, then the pet could be displaying a symptom of pain. A dog in pain may stare at an inanimate object or wall. Sometimes the ears will be pulled back toward the neck.

The head and face of the dog have many means to display symptoms of pain but the body of the animal can also reveal symptoms. Owners should note the overall stance of the dog. A dog normally stands with equal weight on all four feet and the spine in a relatively normal or neutral position. If an animal is standing in a hunched position with the center of the spine being the highest point, then it could indicate that the animal is having abdominal or spinal pain. The contraction of the back muscle removes a small amount of pressure on the spine and/or abdominal organs, providing the pet with a minimal amount of pain relief when standing in a hunched position. If a dog consistently stares or fixates on a body part, then they could be in pain in that area. A dog with pain in the abdomen may look at its stomach periodically or it may consistently lick an area or leg. Pet owners of sick or senior pets should run their hands over their pet's back, neck and limbs daily to check for swellings and monitor the pet's reaction to touch. A pet should be able to withstand mild pressure while being touched on the abdomen and limbs. An animal is likely experiencing pain in an area if he or she cannot tolerate the amount of pressure required to bruise an apple when being palpated over part of their body. The overall movement and activity level of the pet should be monitored daily. If a pet seems restless or shifts positions every few minutes, then he or she may be painful and unable to find a position to alleviate the discomfort. An increase in panting may indicate that a dog is in pain. If a dog has been resting in a cool environment yet he or she is still panting heavily, then the increased effort may be indicating pain rather than increased internal temperature. The normal breathing rate for dogs is 20-30 breaths per minute. This is approximately one breath every other second. If your pet is breathing once every second, then their breathing rate would be considered elevated. An elevated heart rate can indicate pain in dogs. The resting heart rate for small dogs (10-40 pounds) is about 120-150 beats per minute. Larger dogs have slower heart rates and are normally 75-120 beats per minute. An owner can locate the heartbeat by feeling the front lower aspect of the chest just behind the elbow. In large chested dogs it may be difficult to feel the heart beat, but a pet owner can purchase an inexpensive stethoscope at any national drug store.

A dog's hind end and tail can demonstrate symptoms of pain. Reluctance to urinate or defecate can indicate pain in the urinary system, genital area, or colon. A dog with a painful spine or abdomen may be hesitant to position themselves for defecation to avoid discomfort. The tail position can deviate from its normal position when a dog is in pain. A dog that normally holds its tail high may keep it lowered or tucked. A painful dog is often less interested in grooming and an owner may notice an increase in fecal debris and matted hair.

Knowing symptoms of pain in animals will be useful for pet owners interested in maintaining comfort and quality of life in geriatric or critically ill pets. Evaluating an animal's pain in a systematic head to tail manner allows the owner to thoroughly assess their pet for pain in the home environment and permits better communication with their veterinarian.

SYMPTOMS OF PAIN IN THE DOG

HIND END/ TAIL	**BODY/LIMBS**	**HEAD**
Reduced urination/ defecation	Hunched stance/ uneven weight distribution on limbs	Change in vocalizing
Avoids defecation posture	Fixation/licking an area of the body	Increased salivation/drooling
Change in tail position	Sensitivity to palpation	Reduced Appetite
decreased hygiene & grooming	Restless/changing positions frequently	Dilation of pupils in bright light
	↑ heart or breathing rates	Change in ear position

The following worksheet is a pain assessment chart for dogs. It may be beneficial to repeat this assessment on every 15-30 days depending on the severity of your dog's medical condition. The assessment is presented several times to allow for comparison in pain levels at different points in time. Use the total number of YES responses to decide if your dog's pain level is increasing or decreasing.

Is your Dog in Pain?

Pain Assessment 1   **Date:**_____

Pain Symptom	*Yes*	*No*
Has your dog had a sudden increase or decrease in barking?		
Has your dog shown an increase in whimpering or groaning?		
Is your dog demonstrating an increase in drooling or saliva formation?		
Is your dog's appetite reduced?		
Are your dog's pupils large or dilated even in bright light?		
Is your dog breathing rapidly or panting even when he or she is kept in a cool environment?		
Does your dog have a hunched overall stance?		
Does your dog limp or have a change in his or her gait? (may appear to be walking on egg shells)		
Is your dog fixating on or licking a specific part of their body or limbs?		
Does your dog have a reaction when you touch or palpate any part of his or her body? (pressure applied should be just enough to bruise an apple)		
Does your pet appear to be restless or shift positions frequently?		
Does your dog have difficulty defecating or urinating?		
Has your dog demonstrated a change in tail position?		
Does your dog have a reduced ability to maintain hygiene and grooming?		

Each YES maybe an indication that your dog is experiencing pain.

Count the number of YES answers. If you have several YES

answers, then it is very likely that your dog is experiencing pain

and discomfort

number of YES Responses _____

Is your Dog in Pain?

Pain Assessment 2   **Date:**_____

Pain Symptom	*Yes*	*No*
Has your dog had a sudden increase or decrease in barking?		
Has your dog shown an increase in whimpering or groaning?		
Is your dog demonstrating an increase in drooling or saliva formation?		
Is your dog's appetite reduced?		
Are your dog's pupils large or dilated even in bright light?		
Is your dog breathing rapidly or panting even when he or she is kept in a cool environment?		
Does your dog have a hunched overall stance?		
Does your dog limp or have a change in his or her gait? (may appear to be walking on egg shells)		
Is your dog fixating on or licking a specific part of their body or limbs?		
Does your dog have a reaction when you touch or palpate any part of his or her body? (pressure applied should be just enough to bruise an apple)		
Does your pet appear to be restless or shift positions frequently?		
Does your dog have difficulty defecating or urinating?		
Has your dog demonstrated a change in tail position?		
Does your dog have a reduced ability to maintain hygiene and grooming?		

Each YES maybe an indication that your dog is experiencing pain. Count the number of YES answers. If you have several YES answers, then it is very likely that your dog is experiencing pain and discomfort

number of YES Responses _____

Is your Dog in Pain?

Pain Assessment 3   **Date:**_____

Pain Symptom	*Yes*	*No*
Has your dog had a sudden increase or decrease in barking?		
Has your dog shown an increase in whimpering or groaning?		
Is your dog demonstrating an increase in drooling or saliva formation?		
Is your dog's appetite reduced?		
Are your dog's pupils large or dilated even in bright light?		
Is your dog breathing rapidly or panting even when he or she is kept in a cool environment?		
Does your dog have a hunched overall stance?		
Does your dog limp or have a change in his or her gait? (may appear to be walking on egg shells)		
Is your dog fixating on or licking a specific part of their body or limbs?		
Does your dog have a reaction when you touch or palpate any part of his or her body? (pressure applied should be just enough to bruise an apple)		
Does your pet appear to be restless or shift positions frequently?		
Does your dog have difficulty defecating or urinating?		
Has your dog demonstrated a change in tail position?		
Does your dog have a reduced ability to maintain hygiene and grooming?		

Each YES maybe an indication that your dog is experiencing pain.
Count the number of YES answers. If you have several YES
answers, then it is very likely that your dog is experiencing pain
and discomfort

number of YES Responses _____

Is your Dog in Pain?

Pain Assessment 4   **Date:**_____

Pain Symptom	*Yes*	*No*
Has your dog had a sudden increase or decrease in barking?		
Has your dog shown an increase in whimpering or groaning?		
Is your dog demonstrating an increase in drooling or saliva formation?		
Is your dog's appetite reduced?		
Are your dog's pupils large or dilated even in bright light?		
Is your dog breathing rapidly or panting even when he or she is kept in a cool environment?		
Does your dog have a hunched overall stance?		
Does your dog limp or have a change in his or her gait? (may appear to be walking on egg shells)		
Is your dog fixating on or licking a specific part of their body or limbs?		
Does your dog have a reaction when you touch or palpate any part of his or her body? (pressure applied should be just enough to bruise an apple)		
Does your pet appear to be restless or shift positions frequently?		
Does your dog have difficulty defecating or urinating?		
Has your dog demonstrated a change in tail position?		
Does your dog have a reduced ability to maintain hygiene and grooming?		

Each YES maybe an indication that your dog is experiencing pain. Count the number of YES answers. If you have several YES answers, then it is very likely that your dog is experiencing pain and discomfort

number of YES Responses _____

Is your Dog in Pain?

Pain Assessment 5   **Date:**_____

Pain Symptom	_Yes_	_No_
Has your dog had a sudden increase or decrease in barking?		
Has your dog shown an increase in whimpering or groaning?		
Is your dog demonstrating an increase in drooling or saliva formation?		
Is your dog's appetite reduced?		
Are your dog's pupils large or dilated even in bright light?		
Is your dog breathing rapidly or panting even when he or she is kept in a cool environment?		
Does your dog have a hunched overall stance?		
Does your dog limp or have a change in his or her gait? (may appear to be walking on egg shells)		
Is your dog fixating on or licking a specific part of their body or limbs?		
Does your dog have a reaction when you touch or palpate any part of his or her body? (pressure applied should be just enough to bruise an apple)		
Does your pet appear to be restless or shift positions frequently?		
Does your dog have difficulty defecating or urinating?		
Has your dog demonstrated a change in tail position?		
Does your dog have a reduced ability to maintain hygiene and grooming?		

Each YES maybe an indication that your dog is experiencing pain.

Count the number of YES answers. If you have several YES

answers, then it is very likely that your dog is experiencing pain

and discomfort

number of YES Responses _____

Recognizing Pain in Cats

Appreciating the symptoms of feline pain can be a difficult task. Cats still rely heavily on their instincts and are solitary, independent creatures by nature. Dogs have the security of the pack formation or family unit to provide protection when they are experiencing illness or pain; therefore, it is often easier to recognize pain in dogs. Cats will often seek secluded areas for isolation when they are uncomfortable to avoid predators or other aggressive felines. The cat's innate urge to remain quiet and isolated when experiencing pain can make it difficult for the pet owner and veterinarian to recognize and quantitate a cat's level of pain.

Symptoms of pain in cats will be discussed in a head to tail manner to provide pet owners a thorough and logical discussion. With each symptom or behavior change described it will be important for the pet owner to compare it to how to cat responded or behaved in the past. If your pet has always been irritable when being touched over certain body parts, then aggression when being petted or palpated would only be considered a symptom if the response was much more dramatic or intense (i.e., the cat resorts to biting much harder then usual or makes unusual vocal sounds).

The first observation a cat owner should make to asses pain in their pet is the animal's overall attitude and behavior. Cats in pain will often be difficult to find in the house. They may seek new hiding areas and toys/treats may no longer encourage them out of their refuge. Once found, the cat may be abnormally aggressive if the owner attempts to retrieve the cat from the hiding space. This may be due to the fact that pain increases from the pressure of the owner's hands on the cat's body or because the cat is fearful that pain will increase if they are forced to move. Pet owners may also notice that their cat will try to evade touch and attention more frequently when they are uncomfortable. A painful cat may have a dull or depressed attitude and can display a reduced appetite. The overall attitude and behavior of the cat is an important indicator of pain and can provide the pet owner with valuable information regarding their cat's level of comfort.

Feline facial expressions and changes in vocalization can be used to recognize pain in cats. A painful cat will often contract their eyelids and have a squinted appearance. The brow may be furrowed and it may appear that it requires significant effort for the cat to keep its eyes squinted. A painful cat will often hold its head downward so that its eyes look directly at the surface it is lying on, this position maybe an effort to reduce pain and pressure that is occurring in the face or head. When a painful cat does have its eyes open it will often have a blank or glassy eyed stare and be less observant of his or her environment. Cats can have an increase or decrease in vocalization if they are experiencing pain. A cat that historically vocalized with meows and purrs when it experiences pleasure will generally reduce or cease vocalization when they are uncomfortable. Other cats will display pain by dramatically increasing the volume and amount of their vocalization. These cats will display a notable change in their vocalization pattern and may produce long deep meows, groans, growls, or hiss sounds. The pet owner will also find it valuable to assess purring in their cat. Most people associate purring as a behavior that indicates comfort and satisfaction in cats and it may be surprising to discover that in some instances purring can be a symptom of pain. When deciding if a cat's purring is an indicator of pleasure or pain, it will be important to evaluate the volume and consistency of the cat's purr. A happy cat experiencing pleasure will purr loudly and the volume may increase or decrease frequently. The cat may start and stop purring as it rubs its body and scent on objects or people. A painful cat will often purr very softly while lying still. The purr will be consistent as they lay still, and the cat is not dependent on human attention to continue the sound. A painful cat will often purr continuously with a steady volume and intensity. Pet owners can gain valuable information from changes in their cat's facial expression, head position, and vocalization.

The cat's body or trunk has several ways to express pain symptoms. A painful cat will often elect to rest on its breast bone or sternum and will keep all four feet tightly tucked under its body. This may be an effort to reduce back or abdominal pain and it may allow the lungs to expand more easily. A cat that is experiencing pain in a specific area may elect to chew or over groom that area. The cat may also display lameness or a subtle change in their gait or movement. A cat that normally jumps to high places may elect to avoid those places, or it may find a way to reach elevated surfaces that do not require a leap. Monitoring for changes in heart rate and respiration rate will be an important measure that pet owners can use to recognize pain in their cat. Both respiration and heart rate will increase when a cat is pain. The normal respiration rate for a cat sitting comfortably is 16 to 30 breaths per minute. Cats will normally breathe with their mouth closed and have a very subtle rise in their chest. A cat that is breathing rapidly with large movement in their chest is either experiencing pain or difficulty breathing. A normal resting heart rate in a cat is about 120-130 beats per minute. A pet owner can determine their cat's heart rate by holding their cat with one hand cupping the first few ribs. Holding the cat in this manner will allow the owner to feel the heart beat, yet the cat will not be frightened or suspect a medical evaluation is occurring. The owner should count the beats that occur within 6 seconds and then multiply that number by 10. This is the number of heart beats that are occurring in a minute. A heart rate of 160-180 beats per minute could indicate pain or disease and is important information for the pet owner to communicate with their veterinarian. Monitoring feline body position, gait, heart rate, and respiration rate will provide the pet owner opportunities to recognize symptoms of pain in their cat.

The hind end of the cat can display signs of pain. Cats in pain will often begin to have difficulty utilizing the litter box. Most litter boxes have edges that are 4 to 5 inches tall which require cats to lift and flex their front and hind legs to enter the box. Cats with abdominal, back, or orthopedic pain may find it too difficult or painful to attempt to enter the litter box and will begin to defecate outside the box. The pet owner may initially perceive the inappropriate defecation as a behavioral problem, but if it is a sudden change in the cat's normal defecation behavior then it is important to consider that it may be a symptom of pain. A litter box with a very low edge (2in) can be provided to encourage normal litter box behavior. Tail position can provide a pet owner insight about their cat's comfort. Most alert, content cats will walk around with their tail erect and the tip may be bent. A cat that is in pain or feeling ill will often hold their tail down or flat. Grooming and hygiene may be significantly reduced when a cat is in pain. An owner may observe reduced grooming time, increase hair mats, or feces may accumulate on the hind end because the cat is too uncomfortable to clean his or her rectal area. Litter box behavior, tail position, and changes in hygiene can indicate to a pet owner that their cat is experiencing pain.

A pet owner that is aware of the subtle cues that their cat is in pain will have more success communicating with their veterinarian and providing their pet relief. Recognizing pain is an important step in evaluating an animal's quality of life and can help the pet owner with the difficult decision of euthanasia.

The following figure outlines feline

pain symptoms in a head to tail manner

Symptoms of Pain in the Cat

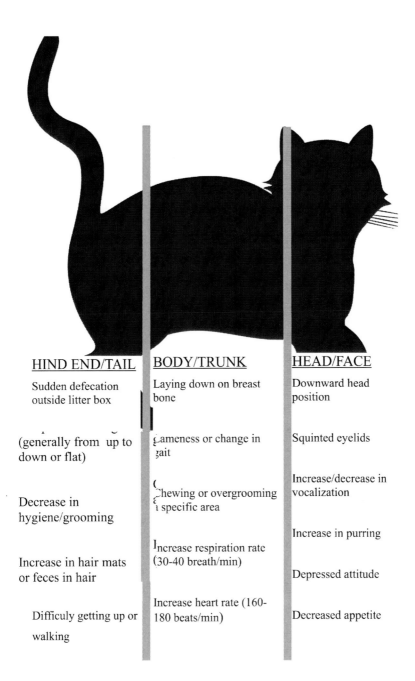

HIND END/TAIL

Sudden defecation outside litter box

(generally from up to down or flat)

Decrease in hygiene/grooming

Increase in hair mats or feces in hair

Difficuly getting up or walking

BODY/TRUNK

Laying down on breast bone

Lameness or change in gait

Chewing or overgrooming a specific area

Increase respiration rate (30-40 breath/min)

Increase heart rate (160-180 beats/min)

HEAD/FACE

Downward head position

Squinted eyelids

Increase/decrease in vocalization

Increase in purring

Depressed attitude

Decreased appetite

The following worksheet is a pain assessment chart for cats. It may be beneficial to repeat this assessment every 15-30 days depending on the severity of your cat's medical condition. The assessment is presented several times to allow for comparison in pain levels at different points in time. Use the total number of YES responses to decide if your cat's pain level is increasing or decreasing.

Is your Cat in Pain?

Pain Assessment 1 **Date:**_____

Pain Symptom	*Yes*	*No*
Does your cat spend more time with his or her head in a downward position?		
Does your cat often have a squinted eye appearance or seem to be straining to keep his or her eyes closed?		
Does your cat have a glassy eyed gaze?		
Has there been a sudden change in the frequency or tone of your cat's vocalization?		
Have you noticed an increase in your cat's purring?		
Does your cat have a reduced appetite?		
Has your cat been spending more time laying down particularly with his or her weight on their breast bone and feet tucked tightly under their body?		
Does your cat limp or have a change in his or her gait? (may appear to be walking on egg shells)		
Is your cat chewing on or licking a specific part of their body or limbs?		
Does your cat have an increase in breaths taken per minute?		
Does your cat have an increase in heart beats per minute?		
Has your cat suddenly started defecating or urinating outside the litter box?		
Has your cat demonstrated a change in tail position?		
Does your cat have a reduced ability to maintain hygiene and grooming?		

Each YES is an indication that your cat is likely experiencing pain. Count the number of YES answers. If you have several YES answers, then it is very likely that your cat is experiencing pain and discomfort

number of YES Responses _____

Is your Cat in Pain?

Pain Assessment 2   **Date:**_____

Pain Symptom	*Yes*	*No*
Does your cat spend more time with his or her head in a downward position?		
Does your cat often have a squinted eye appearance or seem to be straining to keep his or her eyes closed?		
Does your cat have a glassy eyed gaze?		
Has there been a sudden change in the frequency or tone of your cat's vocalization?		
Have you noticed an increase in your cat's purring?		
Does your cat have a reduced appetite?		
Has your cat been spending more time laying down particularly with his or her weight on their breast bone and feet tucked tightly under their body?		
Does your cat limp or have a change in his or her gait? (may appear to be walking on egg shells)		
Is your cat chewing on or licking a specific part of their body or limbs?		
Does your cat have an increase in breaths taken per minute?		
Does your cat have an increase in heart beats per minute?		
Has your cat suddenly started defecating or urinating outside the litter box?		
Has your cat demonstrated a change in tail position?		
Does your cat have a reduced ability to maintain hygiene and grooming?		

Each YES is an indication that your cat is likely experiencing pain. Count the number of YES answers. If you have several YES answers, then it is very likely that your cat is experiencing pain and discomfort

number of YES Responses _____

Is your Cat in Pain?

Pain Assessment 3   **Date:**_____

Pain Symptom	*Yes*	*No*
Does your cat spend more time with his or her head in a downward position?		
Does your cat often have a squinted eye appearance or seem to be straining to keep his or her eyes closed?		
Does your cat have a glassy eyed gaze?		
Has there been a sudden change in the frequency or tone of your cat's vocalization?		
Have you noticed an increase in your cat's purring?		
Does your cat have a reduced appetite?		
Has your cat been spending more time laying down particularly with his or her weight on their breast bone and feet tucked tightly under their body?		
Does your cat limp or have a change in his or her gait? (may appear to be walking on egg shells)		
Is your cat chewing on or licking a specific part of their body or limbs?		
Does your cat have an increase in breaths taken per minute?		
Does your cat have an increase in heart beats per minute?		
Has your cat suddenly started defecating or urinating outside the litter box?		
Has your cat demonstrated a change in tail position?		
Does your cat have a reduced ability to maintain hygiene and grooming?		

Each YES is an indication that your cat is likely experiencing pain. Count the number of YES answers. If you have several YES answers, then it is very likely that your cat is experiencing pain and discomfort

number of YES Responses _____

Is your Cat in Pain?

Pain Assessment 4   **Date:**_____

Pain Symptom	*Yes*	*No*
Does your cat spend more time with his or her head in a downward position?		
Does your cat often have a squinted eye appearance or seem to be straining to keep his or her eyes closed?		
Does your cat have a glassy eyed gaze?		
Has there been a sudden change in the frequency or tone of your cat's vocalization?		
Have you noticed an increase in your cat's purring?		
Does your cat have a reduced appetite?		
Has your cat been spending more time laying down particularly with his or her weight on their breast bone and feet tucked tightly under their body?		
Does your cat limp or have a change in his or her gait? (may appear to be walking on egg shells)		
Is your cat chewing on or licking a specific part of their body or limbs?		
Does your cat have an increase in breaths taken per minute?		
Does your cat have an increase in heart beats per minute?		
Has your cat suddenly started defecating or urinating outside the litter box?		
Has your cat demonstrated a change in tail position?		
Does your cat have a reduced ability to maintain hygiene and grooming?		

Each YES is an indication that your cat is likely experiencing pain. Count the number of YES answers. If you have several YES answers, then it is very likely that your cat is experiencing pain and discomfort

number of YES Responses _____

Is your Cat in Pain?

Pain Assessment 5   **Date:**_____

Pain Symptom	*Yes*	*No*
Does your cat spend more time with his or her head in a downward position?		
Does your cat often have a squinted eye appearance or seem to be straining to keep his or her eyes closed?		
Does your cat have a glassy eyed gaze?		
Has there been a sudden change in the frequency or tone of your cat's vocalization?		
Have you noticed an increase in your cat's purring?		
Does your cat have a reduced appetite?		
Has your cat been spending more time laying down particularly with his or her weight on their breast bone and feet tucked tightly under their body?		
Does your cat limp or have a change in his or her gait? (may appear to be walking on egg shells)		
Is your cat chewing on or licking a specific part of their body or limbs?		
Does your cat have an increase in breaths taken per minute?		
Does your cat have an increase in heart beats per minute?		
Has your cat suddenly started defecating or urinating outside the litter box?		
Has your cat demonstrated a change in tail position?		
Does your cat have a reduced ability to maintain hygiene and grooming?		

Each YES is an indication that your cat is likely experiencing pain. Count the number of YES answers. If you have several YES answers, then it is very likely that your cat is experiencing pain and discomfort

number of YES Responses _____

"The purity of a person's heart can
be measured in how they care for animals."
<u>Anonymous</u>

Chapter 5

How Do I Decide and Live With My Decision?

Chapter 5: How do I decide on euthanasia and live with my decision?

At this point you have established the animal perspective of life and death, understand euthanasia as a medical procedure, and you have learned important measures to recognize animal pain. You will need to combine this information with a thorough understanding of your pet's unique personality and medical condition to know "when it's time" to pursue euthanasia for your friend. There are three major categories of animals that may require euthanasia: the young pet with a serious medical issue, the senior pet with terminal illness, and the senior pet without terminal illness. Each category will be discussed individually to best cater to specific situations that pet owners will face.

Note: only euthanasia for medical purposes will be discussed, euthanasia for behavior reasons (aggression, destructive anxiety, etc.) are not discussed in this book. If you need advice on treating inappropriate animal behaviors find the nearest veterinarian specializing in behavior medicine. A database of board certified specialists can be found at http://dacvb.org

The Young Pet with Serious Medical Issue(s):

When most people picture a "young" pet they imagine an energetic, playful animal with the majority of its expected lifespan ahead. Since all animals and breeds do not age at the same rate we will consider a "young" animal in this discussion to be a dog or cat in the first half of its life. For example, a "young" cat or Chihuahua would be six years old or less but a "young" Great Dane would be three years old or less. Experience in the veterinary field has taught me that animals in this stage of their life have a remarkable healing capacity. Young dogs and cats can suffer from severe infections, ingestion of foreign objects, trauma induced from being hit by a car, or genetic conditions. Despite the severity of these conditions young animals can recover in some instances.

The first step in deciding to treat or euthanize a young animal with a serious medical problem is to obtain an understanding of the **medical condition**. In an emergency, you will often be relying on a veterinarian for this understanding. If you find yourself in this situation be sure to ask the vet any and all questions needed for you to fully understand your animal's medical condition. For example, if a puppy is diagnosed with a parvo virus infection it is important to understand that the virus runs its course in the intestines. The infection causes a shedding of the lining of the intestines which prevents the body from absorbing water and nutrients from the digestive tract. Ultimately, it is not the virus that endangers the animal's life; it is severe dehydration and malnourishment the puppy faces while the intestines repair the damage caused by the virus. An owner that fully comprehends how parvo affects their puppy will understand that treatment needs to be directed at maintaining hydration and nutrition. Your veterinarian will explain that hydration in the face of parvo virus is best managed with IV fluids and medications in the vet hospital, and as an informed owner you will recognize the potential survival your puppy will have with this treatment. Some medical conditions will allow an owner more time to inform themselves. When the situation permits, pet owners should educate themselves via books on pet diseases or trust worthy internet sources. As with any topic, there is a significant amount of misinformation about pet illness on the internet. A reliable internet source written and regulated by veterinarians is the pet library found at www.veterinarypartner.com. Here one can find information on diseases, pet behavior, and medications that will enhance the communication between pet owner and veterinarian. Understanding your pet's **medical condition** will allow you to evaluate the treatment options your veterinarian will present and can help pet owners on a financial budget understand the value in the suggested treatments.

The second step in your decision making process is to understand the **prognosis** of your animal's condition. A prognosis is a prediction of the outcome of an illness or injury. Most vets will give this in terms of a percentage or statistic, and a veterinarian decides on a prognosis based on facts from textbooks and the clinical experience they have had in the past when treating this condition or injury. Here is an example of the importance of comprehending the prognosis of your pet's condition.

Mr. John Doe has a 1 year old dog named Fluffy. Fluffy was hit by a car and one of his back legs was damaged. The vet discovered a break in the bone with an x-ray and explains that surgery will be necessary for Fluffy to survive. The vet also states that there are two surgical options: placing pins into the fracture to bring the bones back together (cost $1200) or amputation (cost$1000). Without a prognosis of each surgical outcome, it seems the surgery to pins the bones in place is optimal as it saves Fluffy's leg and is only slightly more expensive. Discovering the prognosis of the pinning surgery may completely change the decision making process in this case. The vet explains that it is possible to pin the fracture with one surgery, but due to the severity of the fracture there is only a 50% chance that the surgery will allow Fluffy to have function in the leg without chronic pain. If Mr. Doe only has the financial resources for one surgery, then the pinning procedure with a 50% failure rate may be too risky for Fluffy's future. Mr. Doe is sure to ask his vet how dog's handle rear leg amputations. He discovers that 99% of dogs with rear limb amputations recover in 2 weeks, adapt to the limb loss rapidly, and go on to live a happy life. There is no right or wrong answer for Mr. Doe, but when he understood the prognosis of each treatment option he was more prepared to make a decision for Fluffy. This just an example that highlights how a proper understanding of your pet's prognosis will provide confidence that you are making the best decision for your pet and family.

Making decisions regarding a young pet that is critically ill will always be difficult. The animal's medical condition and prognosis may be severe enough that even with the best treatment the pet is predicted to experience significant suffering with little chance of survival. With the medical condition and prognosis understood, you will have to ask yourself several additional questions to make the best decision for your pet. What can you financially commit to the situation? If the pet survives, will there be any permanent disabilities or pain? If the pet recovers is it possible for the condition to reoccur? Will the pet require long term medications or special care? A worksheet for answering these questions is available in the appendix. The following figure is a pictorial representation of the decision making process.

Questions when considering a Young Pet with Serious Medical Issues

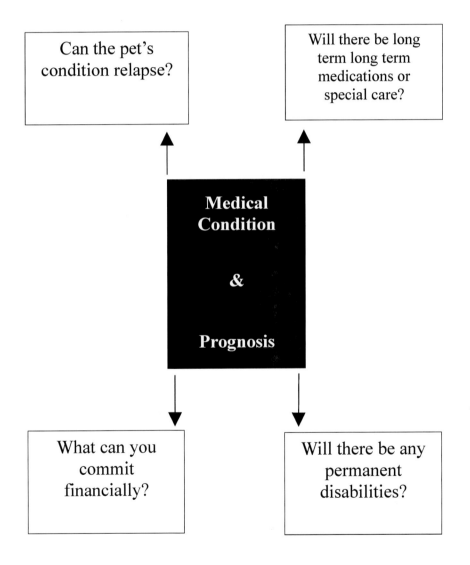

Can the pet's condition relapse?

Will there be long term long term medications or special care?

Medical Condition

&

Prognosis

What can you commit financially?

Will there be any permanent disabilities?

If you find yourself in this situation it is encouraged that you trust your veterinarian's advice and recommendations. Speaking from the perspective of the vet, one of the most tragic outcomes is the unnecessary euthanasia of a young animal. Veterinarians realize the healing capacity of the young animal and will generally assist the pet owner in pursuing treatment if that is in the best interest of the animal. In emergency situations, a vet clinic may accept various credit forms such as CareCredit®, may design a treatment plan in-line with an owner's financial budget, or the clinic may accept a down payment with a monthly payment schedule for long standing clients. If you find that your veterinarian is suggesting euthanasia as the primary option for the animal, it is advised that you take note of this suggestion. Again, it is against the nature of the veterinarian to suggest euthanasia of the young animal unless he or she is thoroughly convinced that the potential suffering of the animal greatly exceeds the likelihood of survival. Speaking from personal experience, the only thing worse than euthanizing a young animal is watching a young animal suffer with little to no hope of recovery. When you combine an understanding of your pet's medical condition and prognosis with open, honest communication between you and your veterinarian you will be confident that you are making a compassionate and humane decision for your young pet.

Please refer to the Appendix on page 102 to fill out the form regarding your pet's medical condition. The form will guide you through the process of understanding your pet's condition and will ensure that you ask your vet all the proper question

The Senior Pet with Terminal Illness:

If you are a pet owner in this situation, then you are faced with managing your pet's illness and discomfort while realizing there will be a point in time when therapies and medications can no longer maintain your pet's comfort . Pets in this category may suffer from cancer, metabolic disease (examples are diabetes and thyroid disease), organ failure, or autoimmune/genetic diseases. As in the decision making for young pets, understanding your pet's medical condition and prognosis is essential. Serious illness or injury in a young pet is generally an emergency situation and owners often have very little time in which to make important decisions. Generally, pet owners of senior dogs and cats diagnosed with terminal disease will have at least a few days or weeks to inform themselves of their pet's condition and options.

The most essential advice for pet owners in this situation is to **be informed** and **be prepared**. You will likely have regular visits and communication with your veterinarian. Utilize your vet's time effectively in your appointments. When I worked in the hospital setting, it was often very helpful when owners with terminally ill pets kept brief logs of their pet's condition/activities when at home. It was just as helpful when the owner had written down questions they had acquired since our last visit. The best pet owners did research on their pet's disease via books, the internet (www.veterinarypartner.com), and discussions with other pet owners. It is important for the pet owner to discuss what they learn about their pet's disease with their veterinarian in a polite, non-argumentative manner. A compassionate and thorough veterinarian is essential for prolonging your pet's life, and he or she is likely one of the greatest advocates for your pet. They will want to do everything possible to manage the illness and keep your pet comfortable. If you discover a treatment option or medication that your veterinarian has not yet suggested, then present the information you have found in a polite, professional manner. Vets go to yearly educational conferences to maintain their license to practice medicine, but it impossible to stay on top of every new discovery and medication for every disease and every animal all the time. If the information or medication has the potential to help your pet without causing harmful side effects, then your pet's doctor will generally be open to the new treatment.

A part of becoming an informed pet owner of a senior animal with a terminal illness is researching and understanding the human experience of your pet's disease. There are very few diseases that animals acquire exclusively; most terminal illnesses that animals experience are also diagnosed in human medicine. It often surprises pet owners that people and animals can suffer the same disease process, but people and animals share the same organs that can fail or develop cancer. An owner that develops an understanding of the human experience of their pet's disease will have more insight on their pet's pain and comfort level. I began to appreciate the importance of the pet owner's understanding of how humans experience their pet's disease after a phone conversation with a Home Farewell client. One morning I received a call from a woman that had a cat suffering from osteosarcoma (bone cancer). The cat had been battling this cancer for six months and had seemed to maintain a reasonable quality of life until the night prior. The cat was reluctant to eat a meal the night prior to her phone call, and he was barely interested in breakfast that morning. The pet was still able to get around the house and purred when begin caressed by the owner. The woman was struggling to decide if euthanasia was the right decision at this point for her pet. Her veterinarian had told her once cats are diagnosed with osteosarcoma they generally have a 6 month life expectancy and that loss of appetite or limping would be symptoms that the pet was nearing the end. The woman trusted her vet's advice but was very distraught because her cat seemed to be so content when resting and being caressed. In my efforts to help the woman in her decision making process, I inadvertently mentioned information I had learned about the human experience of osteosarcoma. During our conversation, I mentioned that osteosarcoma can be one of the most painful cancers a human can experience, and even with the strongest pain medications the person's pain is often still very intense. We also discussed that cat's have a very strong instinct to hide illness and pain where as humans can express their pain without fear of attack by a predator or rejection from their species. Pets likely experience an equal level of pain when compared to humans suffering the same condition, even if they are following their instincts to reduce their display of suffering. At this point in our conversation, the woman seemed to experience significant clarity and the weight of the decision had been lifted from her. She found comparing the human and cat experience of osteosarcoma very helpful, and it provided her confidence in making medical decisions for her cat. Our animals cannot talk to us and we are reliant on their behavior and body language to evaluate their comfort level. Developing an understanding of the human experience of your pet's condition can be a tool to gain insight on your pet's quality of life.

While it is important to be informed and understand what your pet will be going through, it is equally important to **be prepared** for the point in time when there are no longer treatment options or medications to keep your pet comfortable. In my experience with Home Farewell, the clients that seem to have the best coping skills when dealing with senior pets suffering from terminal illness were individuals that educated themselves on their pet's disease allowing them to create parameters for end of life decisions. For instance, an owner that has an animal with bladder cancer will know that their pet's cancer does not run the risk of spreading to other organs but will continue to grow in the bladder until the pet cannot pass urine. This pet owner may decide that 12 hours without the ability to urinate is a humane parameter to help them with their pet's end of life decisions. A cat in kidney failure will often struggle with their appetite for food. Fluids given under the skin along with medicine to increase appetite can encourage eating, but the cat may eventually lose its appetite completely. A pet owner that understands these circumstances may decide that the inability to eat for 24 hours is a parameter for deciding euthanasia. Your veterinarian will be able to assist you on defining parameters for your pet's terminal illness. Outlining parameters to define your pet's quality of life in advance will ensure that you are able to make the best decision for your pet. When your pet's condition begins to deteriorate you will likely experience significant emotional distress and sadness, but having a rational decision making plan in place will provide tremendous benefit.

Owners of senior pets with terminal illness will benefit by preparing their pet's end of life decisions in advance. Having the parameters set to measure their pet's quality of life is very important, but it is also important to make as many end of life decisions as possible in advance. It is always difficult and there are many options, but making the decisions before the pet's health deteriorates will be easier for the pet owner. Do you want the euthanasia performed at home or in the clinic? If you prefer the home environment be sure to locate a veterinarian that performs home euthanasia in advance. A national directory of veterinarians providing this service can be found at www.inhomepeteuthanasia.com. Call in advance to learn about the veterinarian's scheduling system and make sure you are comfortable with their demeanor and method for performing the procedure. If you prefer the clinic setting, discuss how your vet generally handles euthanasia appointments. Some clinics have separate rooms designed to be comforting and relaxing for euthanasia appointments, some have separate entrances and exits for grieving owners, and some clinics will have clients pre-pay or will send a bill in the mail so clients do not have to stand in the checkout line. It is advised to make decisions regarding your pet's remains in advance as well. Pet owners that are prepared will likely find it comforting to have made their pet's end of life decisions in advance.

For any pet owner, learning that their beloved friend has a terminal condition is one of their biggest fears. Informing yourself on your pet's condition, developing an understanding of the human experience of your pet's condition, setting parameters in advance to define your pet's quality of life, and making end of life decisions before your pet's health deteriorates can impart an owner with the strength and courage to help their pet through this process.

Please refer to the Appendix on page 102 to fill out the form regarding your pet's medical condition. The form will guide you through the process of understanding your pet's condition and will ensure that you ask your vet all the proper question

Below is an equation to help owners understanding the decision making process for senior pets with a terminal illness.

Equation for the Senior Pet with Terminal Illness

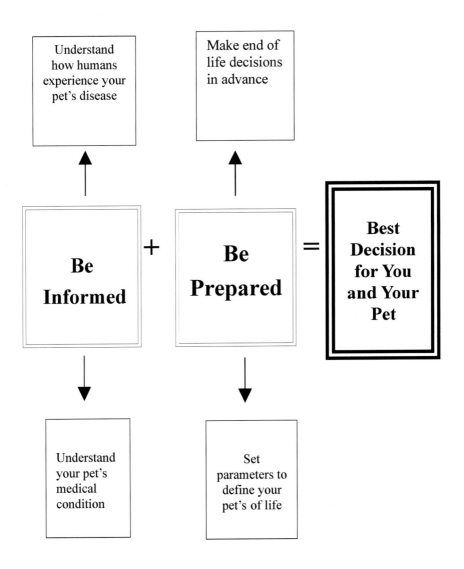

Understand how humans experience your pet's disease

Make end of life decisions in advance

Be Informed + **Be Prepared** = **Best Decision for You and Your Pet**

Understand your pet's medical condition

Set parameters to define your pet's of life

The Senior Pet Without Terminal Illness:

Pets in this category have generally met or exceeded their predicted lifespan. They do not suffer from one major illness, but have multiple health concerns related to the age of their body. Their spirit and mental capabilities are often well intact, but their body seems to be a shell that is crumbling and failing them in multiple areas. This situation seems to be the most difficult for pet owners. Making end of life decisions for pets in this condition can be an overwhelming experience for most individuals. There is nothing that can be said that will reduce the burden and emotional strain that an owner will face when their pet is in this state, but one can approach this decision with more confidence and strength with the right perspective.

As we watch our senior pets struggle with mobility, lose the desire to groom, or become incontinent it is all too easy to compare them to ourselves or a loved one in the final stages of their life. In our current society, end of life decisions for humans is a very controversial subject. There are concerns that health care options will be restricted or rationed due to the age of the human patient, and there are religious and legal influences that denounce ending human life prematurely. This book is not designed to cover human end of life decisions, and I feel that it is not healthy to compare human and animal end of life decisions in the same discussion. I personally find it much easier to make end of life decisions for animals with the mindset that they are "animals/pets." Pet owners will find Chapter 2 of this book: Human and Animal Perspectives of Life and Death essential to keeping the right mindset to make the best decision for their pet. It is important to remember that animals have no aspiration for living forever and they do not share our deep fear of death.

With the right mindset in place, the owner of a senior pet can ask themselves several questions to assist in deciding the animal's current quality of life. Is your pet interested and able to eat food without pain? When was the last time your pet demonstrated interest in toys or activities they enjoyed earlier in life (fetch, play when interacting with people, going for a walk, cat scratch post, etc) ? Does your pet seem to stare into corners or seemed lost in your house on a daily basis? Has your pet lost the ability to get up and move to use the bathroom or eat food? Has your pet lost the ability to control urination and/or defecation? Answering these questions can help pet owners define the overall quality of their senior pet's life.

An owner that maintains the animal perspective of aging/death and answers questions to assess their animal's quality of life may also find it helpful to incorporate their pet's overall personality into the decision making process. To best explain how important your pet's overall personality can be when considering end of life decisions, we will consider the personalities of my two dogs: Simon and Icarus. They are both male Australian Shepherds but have very different personalities. Simon is a very proud, loyal animal. He feels the needs to protect his family and home. He wants to follow all the household rules, and is very upset when he displeases his family. He is intensely competitive with frisbee catching, and he is happiest when he can accompany his master on daily outings. Icarus is fun loving and lazy. The outdoors are merely a place for going to the bathroom and a quick game of chase. He is not concerned with rules or being reprimanded. He is happiest when he is relaxing with his family on the couch or in bed. If they were to lose their mobility or became incontinent in there senior years, then I would make very different decisions for each of them. If Simon lost the ability to getup on his own or he could not keep himself from urinating in the house, then I would know without a doubt that he would be experiencing remorse and humiliation. Even if he was not in physical pain, I believe he would be emotionally uncomfortable and I will not ask him to remain here for very long in that condition. If Icarus lost mobility or became incontinent, I predict he would enjoy the extra attention and time on the couch. As long as he was not experiencing physical pain, I believe he would be content in that situation. As you can see the personality of the animal can play a major role in the end of life decision making for senior pets.

When a pet does not have a major medical illness there is no medical condition to research and there is no prognosis to understand. It is an extremely difficult situation for the pet owner to face, and at times the responsibility to make end of life decisions for pets in this state will seem overwhelming. Be sure to not allow human end of life controversies to cloud your decision making, and systemically answer questions that can define your pet's quality of life. Most importantly, factor in your pet's personality into your decision making. Following this advice will allow the pet owner to protect their animal from continued physical discomfort and emotional distress, which will ultimately produce a humane decision that is in the best interest of the senior pet.

The following worksheet is designed to help the pet owner assess the senior pet's quality of life. The worksheet is repeated 4 times to allow the pet to be assessed on multiple occasions. The quality of life assessments can be compared to another to measure changes in the pet's health and comfort.

Senior/Sick Pet Quality of Life

Assessment 1

Date of Assessment: _____

Describe your pet's overall personality and favorite activities when he or she was young and healthy:

_____

_____

_____

Quality of Life Questions	Y	N	Effect on Personality	Y	N
Is your pet able to get up and down without assistance?			If No, does the inability to get up and down have a negative effect on your pet's personality?		
Does your pet have a normal appetite?			Did your pet have a love of food and eating when they were healthy and or young?		
Does your pet still play with toys?			Were toys an important part of your pet's youth?		
Is your pet able to go for a brief walk ? (not applicable to cats)			Were walks, hikes, runs, or swimming important to your pet in the past?		
Is your pet able to urinate/defecate without pain?			Does your pet become upset if he or she has "accidents" in the house?		

Is your pet able to greet guests at the door?			Did your pet enjoy protecting the front door and the boundaries of the home?		
Can your pet rest/ sleep comfortably for at least 1 hour?			When young and or healthy did your pet spend most of his or her time sleeping?		
Has your pet lost a sense? (i.e. smell, sight, hearing)			If your pet has lost one of his or her senses, does that limitation have a negative effect on your pet's personality?		
Overall, does your pet have more "bad" days then "good" days?			On your pet's "bad" days does there seem to be a negative effect on his or personality? (you may notice aggression, fear, or a loss of your pet's personality or "spirit")		
Does your pet spend Most of it's time in hiding or in seclusion?			Would it negatively impact your pet's if he or she could not be an active family member?		

.

Take a moment to reflect on the various ways your pet's quality of life is impacting his or her personality.

Overall, would you be happy and content if you were living in your pet's current quality of life. _____ yes _____ No

Additional Notes for this Quality of Life Assessment

_____

_____

_____

Senior/Sick Pet Quality of Life

Assessment 2

Date of Assessment: _____

Describe your pet's overall personality and favorite activities when he or she was young and healthy:

_____

_____

_____

Quality of Life Questions	Y	N	Effect on Personality	Y	N
Is your pet able to get up and down without assistance?			If No, does the inability to get up and down have a negative effect on your pet's personality?		
Does your pet have a normal appetite?			Did your pet have a love of food and eating when they were healthy and or young?		
Does your pet still play with toys?			Were toys an important part of your pet's youth?		
Is your pet able to go for a brief walk ? (not applicable to cats)			Were walks, hikes, runs, or swimming important to your pet in the past?		
Is your pet able to urinate/defecate without pain?			Does your pet become upset if he or she has "accidents" in the house?		

Is your pet able to greet guests at the door?			Did your pet enjoy protecting the front door and the boundaries of the home?		
Can your pet rest/ sleep comfortably for at least 1 hour?			When young and or healthy did your pet spend most of his or her time sleeping?		
Has your pet lost a sense? (i.e. smell, sight, hearing)			If your pet has lost one of his or her senses, does that limitation have a negative effect on your pet's personality?		
Overall, does your pet have more "bad" days then "good" days?			On your pet's "bad" days does there seem to be a negative effect on his or personality? (you may notice aggression, fear, or a loss of your pet's personality or "spirit")		
Does your pet spend Most of it's time in hiding or in seclusion?			Would it negatively impact your pet's if he or she could not be an active family member?		

.

Take a moment to reflect on the various ways your pet's quality of life is impacting his or her personality.

Overall, would you be happy and content if you were living in your pet's current quality of life. _____ yes _____ No

Additional Notes for this Quality of Life Assessment

_____

_____

_____

Senior/Sick Pet Quality of Life

Assessment 3

Date of Assessment: _____

Describe your pet's overall personality and favorite activities when he or she was young and healthy:

_____

_____

_____

Quality of Life Questions	Y	N	Effect on Personality	Y	N
Is your pet able to get up and down without assistance?			If No, does the inability to get up and down have a negative effect on your pet's personality?		
Does your pet have a normal appetite?			Did your pet have a love of food and eating when they were healthy and or young?		
Does your pet still play with toys?			Were toys an important part of your pet's youth?		
Is your pet able to go for a brief walk ? (not applicable to cats)			Were walks, hikes, runs, or swimming important to your pet in the past?		
Is your pet able to urinate/defecate without pain?			Does your pet become upset if he or she has "accidents" in the house?		

Is your pet able to greet guests at the door?		Did your pet enjoy protecting the front door and the boundaries of the home?		
Can your pet rest/ sleep comfortably for at least 1 hour?		When young and or healthy did your pet spend most of his or her time sleeping?		
Has your pet lost a sense? (i.e. smell, sight, hearing)		If your pet has lost one of his or her senses, does that limitation have a negative effect on your pet's personality?		
Overall, does your pet have more "bad" days then "good" days?		On your pet's "bad" days does there seem to be a negative effect on his or personality? (you may notice aggression, fear, or a loss of your pet's personality or "spirit")		
Does your pet spend Most of it's time in hiding or in seclusion?		Would it negatively impact your pet's if he or she could not be an active family member?		

.

Take a moment to reflect on the various ways your pet's quality of life is impacting his or her personality.

Overall, would you be happy and content if you were living in your pet's current quality of life. _____ yes _____ No

Additional Notes for this Quality of Life Assessment

_____

_____

_____

Senior/Sick Pet Quality of Life

Assessment 4

Date of Assessment: _____

Describe your pet's overall personality and favorite activities when he or she was young and healthy:

_____

_____

_____

Quality of Life Questions	Y	N	Effect on Personality	Y	N
Is your pet able to get up and down without assistance?			If No, does the inability to get up and down have a negative effect on your pet's personality?		
Does your pet have a normal appetite?			Did your pet have a love of food and eating when they were healthy and or young?		
Does your pet still play with toys?			Were toys an important part of your pet's youth?		
Is your pet able to go for a brief walk ? (not applicable to cats)			Were walks, hikes, runs, or swimming important to your pet in the past?		
Is your pet able to urinate/defecate without pain?			Does your pet become upset if he or she has "accidents" in the house?		

			Did your pet enjoy protecting the front door and the boundaries of the home?		
Is your pet able to greet guests at the door?			Did your pet enjoy protecting the front door and the boundaries of the home?		
Can your pet rest/ sleep comfortably for at least 1 hour?			When young and or healthy did your pet spend most of his or her time sleeping?		
Has your pet lost a sense? (i.e. smell, sight, hearing)			If your pet has lost one of his or her senses, does that limitation have a negative effect on your pet's personality?		
Overall, does your pet have more "bad" days then "good" days?			On your pet's "bad" days does there seem to be a negative effect on his or personality? (you may notice aggression, fear, or a loss of your pet's personality or "spirit")		
Does your pet spend Most of it's time in hiding or in seclusion?			Would it negatively impact your pet's if he or she could not be an active family member?		

.

Take a moment to reflect on the various ways your pet's quality of life is impacting his or her personality.

Overall, would you be happy and content if you were living in your pet's current quality of life. _____ yes _____ No

Additional Notes for this Quality of Life Assessment

_____

_____

_____

"The cat is the animal to whom the Creator gave the biggest eye, the softest fur, the most supremely delicate nostrils, a mobile ear, an unrivaled paw and a curved claw borrowed from the rose-tree."

Sidonie Gabrielle

Chapter 6

Final Thoughts

Chapter 6: Final Thoughts

Words are not available to make facing farewell with your pet and easy process. Most American households view a pet as a beloved member of the family and end of life decision making can be a very difficult process. At this point you have gained insight on the animal perception of the life cycle, and you understand that your pets do not share our human fear and avoidance of old age and death. You have educated yourself on the procedure of euthanasia, which makes you an informed medical advocate for your pet. You can recognize common ways dogs and cats display pain, allowing you and your veterinarian to work as a team to keep your pet comfortable for the longest amount of time possible.

As a veterinarian and pet owner, it seems that we are not allowed enough years with our best friends. At times, the decade or so we have with our pets is just not long enough. I sometimes find myself frustrated with the short lifespan of our pets as I watch my pets age and as I help families through my Home Farewell euthanasia service. When I find myself resenting the frequency at which we are faced with farewell, I seek comfort in a story that is passed around the veterinary profession. The source of the story is unknown but it surrounds a young boy's perspective on his dog's lifespan. A mother, father, and six-year-old son take their older lab, Jake, to the vet to be put to sleep. Jake suffered from severe arthritis, and he had reached the point where he could no longer get up and down without substantial pain. The vet explained the euthanasia procedure to the parents and knelt down to make sure the young boy understood that Jake was going to sleep permanently so he will no longer be in pain. The vet asked the boy, "Do you understand why we are putting Jake to sleep today?" The boy thought for a moment and said, "Yes, my mom told me we are here in life to learn how to be good. Jake was born good and he loved everyone. He always knew how to be good so he does not need to stay here as long as I do."

The young boy's perspective is unique and refreshing. It reminds pet owners to enjoy and remember the time they have had with their pet, rather than focusing energy on time they do not have with their friend.

You have courageously read through the difficult material in this book in an effort to make the best decision for your pet. Families and individuals that prepare and educate themselves are better equipped to judge the quality of their pet's life and time their pet's euthanasia appropriately. When you are facing farewell with your pet, follow your instincts, your veterinarian's guidance, and advice from this book to make a compassionate decision for your pet that is a final act of love and mercy.

Appendix

Assessment of Your Pet's Medical Condition

Name of Disease:_____

Date of Diagnosis:_____

List Symptoms your pet is currently experiencing:

_____   _____   _____

_____   _____   _____

_____   _____   _____

List symptoms your pet is not currently experiencing but are common with your
pet's medical condition

_____   _____   _____

_____   _____   _____

What diagnostic tests have been performed? (bloodwork, xrays,
ultrasound, biopsy, etc)

_____

_____

_____

Are their any further diagnostic tests needed as your pet's disease
progresses?

_____

_____

_____

List any treatments that your veterinarian recommends that are not medication (accupuncture, Fluids given under the skin, etc)

_____

_____

Your Pet's Medication

MEDICATION	PURPOSE (pain relief, antibiotic, etc)	SIDE EFFECTS

Are their other medications your pet will need to take as their disease progresses?

_____

_____

_____

What is the prognosis of your pet's disease?

_____

_____

_____

_____

_____

_____

Based on your pet's disease, what is his or her life expectancy?

_____

_____

Discuss with your veterinarian changes you will likely notice with your pet that indicate your pet's quality of life is diminishing

_____

_____

_____

_____

_____

_____

_____

_____

_____

Valuable internet resources

National Directory for Home Euthanasia Veterinarians

http://www.inhomepeteuthanasia.com/

Trusted Source for Veterinary Medial Information

http://www.veterinarypartner.com

Pet Loss Support

The Association for Pet Loss and Bereavement

http://aplb.org/index.html

Pet loss grief consultations over the phone

www.petloss.com

Questionaire for Young Pets with Serious Medical Issues

Use this questionaire during your discussion with your veterinarian to help you make the best decision for your pet

How long will it take for your pet to recover?

_____

_____

What is the prognosis (you vet may provide this in a best and worst case scenario)?

_____

_____

_____

What is the predicted cost to get your pet back into the condition to live a happy, comfortable life?

Low end of estimate $_____

High end of estimate $_____

Is there potential for your pet's condition to relapse?

_____

_____

_____

Will your pet have any permanent diabilities, if so please describe?

_____

_____

_____

Will your pet require any longterm treatments or medications, if so please describe?

_____

_____

_____

Additional Notes from the Discussion with your Veterinarian

_____

_____

_____

_____

_____

_____

_____

_____

_____

_____

Setting Parameters for Your Pet

Have a discussuion with your vet and define the paramters for
quality of life based on your pet's medical condition

Your Pet's Diagnosis:_____

Potential changes to your pet that can be used to define quality of life ex: inability to eat for 24 hours, painful upon defecation for 12 hours or more, etc)	Date that you observe this change in your pet

NOTES/PHOTOS OF YOUR PET

NOTES/PHOTOS OF YOUR PET

NOTES/PHOTOS OF YOUR PET